# The Artist's Airbrush Manual

# The Artist's Airbrush Manual
## Clement Marten

**DAVID & CHARLES**
Newton Abbot   London

British Library Cataloguing in Publication Data

Marten, Clement
  The artist's airbrush manual.
  1. Airbrush art
  I. Title
  751.4'94    NC915.A35

ISBN 0-7153-7997-6

Typeset by ABM Typographics Ltd, Hull
Printed in Great Britain
by A Wheaton & Co Ltd, Exeter
for David & Charles (Publishers) Limited
Brunel House Newton Abbot Devon

# Contents

# Introduction

Artists are forever seeking new ways to achieve effects that will give new dimensions to their art. Until the end of the last century, their choice was limited and had been for thousands of years. Early cave artists used only their fingers and pieces of wood with which to create works of art, which endure and are admired to this day. At some time an innovator thought of tying animal hairs on to the end of a twig in order to obtain a more delicate effect than with finger or stick.

As time went on the artist became more proficient with his brush-making and experimented with hairs from different animals, but still did not have a great choice when it came to putting paint to canvas or paper.

That is until Charles Burdick, an artist of some repute and ability, decided that he wished to extend the horizons of his art, but was not satisfied with the options open to him. Although a man of considerable vision, even he could not have foreseen what he was starting when he invented and patented the airbrush, which he named the Aerograph, an instrument for spraying paint, in a controlled manner, on to almost any surface.

In 1893 he formed The Fountain Brush Company and started to manufacture the airbrush in a small factory in Clerkenwell Green, London, England. It was probably no coincidence that his factory was sited in Clerkenwell, at that time the area of London where watch and clockmakers followed their trade, thus providing workers skilled in the production of small precision-made components. In 1900 Mr Burdick founded the Aerograph Company Limited. It so happened that during this period an ear, nose and throat specialist, Dr Allen DeVilbiss of Toledo, USA, was seeking a way of applying medicaments to the throats of his patients as an alternative to using a swab. He developed a spray which proved successful and formed a company to manufacture it in its various forms.

Meanwhile, in London, new applications of the airbrush were being evolved and new variants manufactured including the industrial spray gun.

In 1907 the factory moved to larger premises and the offices to Holborn Viaduct in London and in 1931 the British and American companies amalgamated. Other manufacturers have since produced paint-spraying equipment with variations of design and construction, but still following the original concept. Very few industries do not use spraying techniques to apply paint or other fluids to an infinite variety of surfaces for a multitude of purposes. Paint-spraying has even become computerised, for example in the furniture trade where the paint spray is programmed to follow movements first determined by a human operator. Having been recorded on tape, the signals are fed through the computer, which in turn controls the progress of the spray.

In 1932 I became a studio lad sweeping floors, washing palettes and making tea, but learning to be an airbrusher and photographic retoucher under the guidance of a very talented and experienced artist, Jimmy Hutton, who had been an airbrusher and retoucher before the First World War.

The airbrush provided for me to practise with was made in about 1912; the plating had worn off and the handle was missing, but by practising hour after hour, I became fairly useful in about two years. After five years I reached a stage where I could just about make the airbrush do what I wanted. Now, after forty-five years, I think I may master it yet! This book is designed to guide the embryo airbrusher along the path to proficiency. It may also suggest to the established artist ways of developing skills and techniques which may enable him to produce a greater variety of work. The airbrush, although a comparatively simple instrument, offers immense opportunities for experimentation; even in my advanced years, I am still learning new tricks as a result of undertaking work requiring a new approach.

Although the airbrush is a very useful instrument, do not be tempted to use it when other techniques would be more suitable for the work in hand. There is nothing worse, in my opinion, than the artificial over-smooth appearance of the 'airbrushed look'. Regrettably, the airbrush is sometimes used to attempt to disguise mediocre draughtsmanship; another trap is to use the airbrush when, in all probability, a colour wash would be more suitable. Too easily can character and spontaneity be airbrushed out of a piece of artwork, so use it sparingly.

This book is mainly concerned with the needle-controlled airbrush, but there are other types of paint sprays used by artists, modellers and craftsmen. However, many of the recommendations made apply not only to the needle-controlled instrument, but also to other forms of paint spray.

An appendix lists the products of the leading manufacturers of airbrushes and paint sprays, so that intending purchasers may see the selection available.

I am grateful to the Aerograph-DeVilbiss Company Limited for providing the historical details of the development of the airbrush. Incidentally, airbrushing is frequently referred to as 'Aerographing' just as vacuum cleaning is often called 'Hoovering', regardless of make.

All tone illustrations can only be reproduced in a book with a screen of dots over the image. Because of this technical necessity, it is not possible to reproduce airbrushed examples exactly as the original.

*Clement Marten*

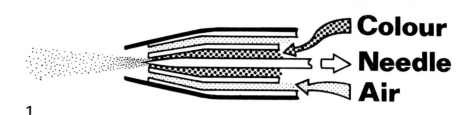

**Colour**
**Needle**
**Air**

1

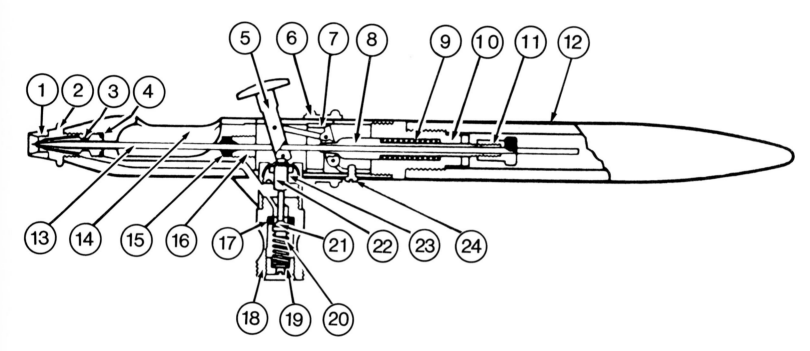

2

| 1 | Air cap guard | 13 | Fluid needle |
| --- | --- | --- | --- |
| 2 | Air cap | 14 | Colour cup/reservoir |
| 3 | Nozzle | 15 | Needle gland washer |
| 4 | Nozzle washer | 16 | Needle packing gland |
| 5 | Lever assembly | 17 | Air valve washer |
| 6 | Cam ring | 18 | Air valve box |
| 7 | Cam | 19 | Air valve spring retainer |
| 8 | Square piece | 20 | Air valve spring |
| 9 | Needle spring | 21 | Air valve stem |
| 10 | Needle spring box | 22 | Diaphragm assembly |
| 11 | Needle locking nut | 23 | Diaphragm nut |
| 12 | Handle | 24 | Fixing screw |

# The airbrush and how it works

**1**

The airbrush works on the principle of external atomisation ; compressed air is allowed to flow past an orifice from which a fluid is drawn by the passage of the air. A partial vacuum occurs at the front of the fluid orifice and this, combined with the pressure of the atmosphere of 14.7psi on the fluid in the reservoir, causes the fluid to flow. The fluid then mixes with the compressed, fast moving air and is atomised into minute droplets.

The character of the resultant spray can be altered by regulating the pressure of air passing the orifice or by regulating the amount of liquid which is allowed to pass through it. In this way, not only is it possible to alter the degree of atomisation of the liquid by the regulation of the flow of air and colour, but also to alter the density of the colour being sprayed on to a surface. Other factors which control density are the strength of the colour before atomisation, the length of time the spray is directed towards the work surface, and the distance between the airbrush and the work surface.

**2**

To be competent in the use of the airbrush, it is helpful to understand how it works and to be familiar with the main component parts and their functions.

The *air cap* and *guard* (1 & 2) through which the compressed air passes to atomise the colour drawn from the fluid nozzle (3). A small circular hole in the centre of the air cap face ensures that the fluid nozzle is accurately centred, but not touching. In this way a thin circular gap is formed between nozzle and air cap allowing a passage for the compressed air. The air cap guard (2), as its name implies, is a protection for the finely shaped delicate needle point (13).

The *nozzle* (3) is a tube, the inside of which is tapered towards the front, ending in a final orifice of 1:12,000in diameter. In this the tapered *fluid needle* (13) moves forward or backwards, so that the two tapers have a combined effect of regulating the flow of liquid from the colour reservoir.

The fluid needle has an accurately ground taper at its forward end, so finely ground that the point is extremely sharp. It is absolutely imperative for this point to be preserved, because it is essential to the good performance of the airbrush (see 'Diagnosis of Faults', page 76).

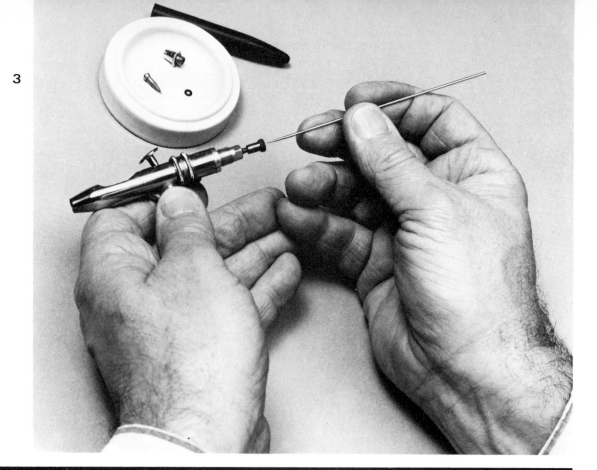

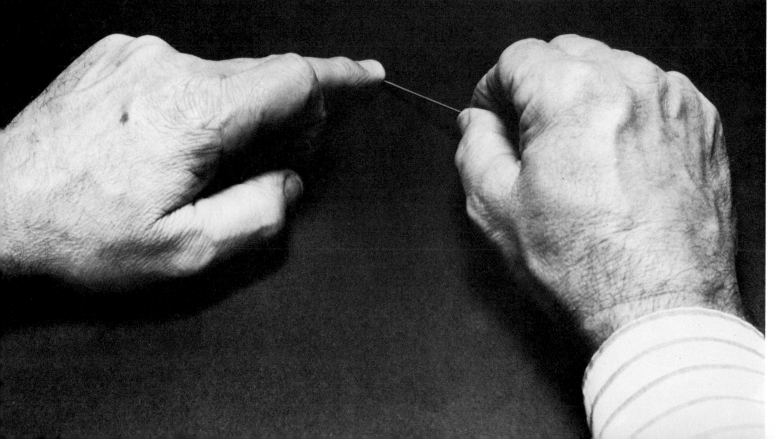

**3** The needle enters the airbrush from the rear, point first, through a tube and is held in place in this tube by the *needle locking nut* (11). The photograph shows a fluid needle being carefully inserted into the rear of the needle locking nut. The *nozzle* (3), *nozzle washer* (4), *air cap* (2) and *guard* (1), seen in the palette, will be assembled into the body of the airbrush before the fluid needle is pushed fully forward. When the fluid needle is seated in the nozzle, the needle locking nut can be tightened.

When replacing the needle, great care should be taken to ensure that the sharp point does not touch any part as it enters the tube and lever assembly (5-7). The finger button at the top of the lever control should be forward.

**4** Should the needle point be bent, the fault can be partially remedied by placing the taper on to a clean, flat surface, putting a finger on top of the taper and then revolving the needle and, at the same time, withdrawing the needle from under the finger. Do this several times. However, it is unlikely that the bent point will ever be entirely straightened, and if the point breaks off, good airbrushing will be difficult to obtain, because it is necessary for the fine point of the needle to protrude through the orifice of the nozzle in order to obtain that degree of perfect atomisation required for fine and accurate work.

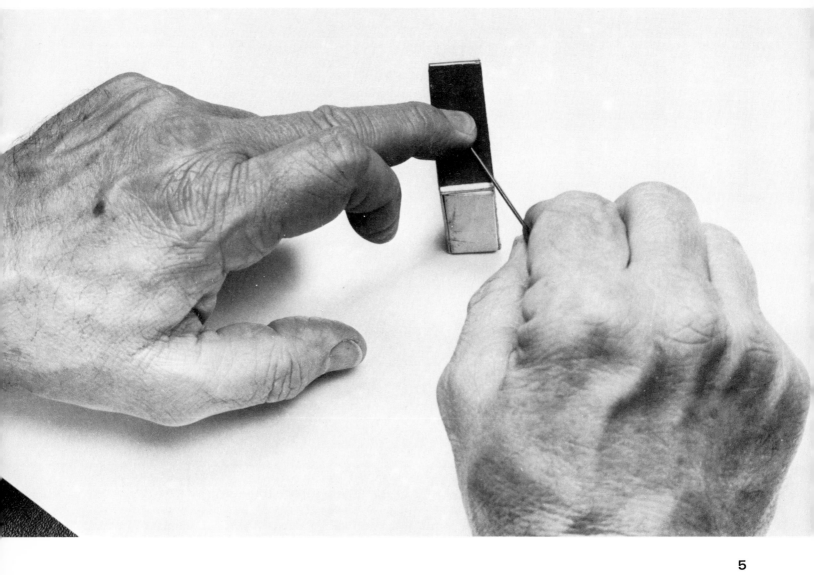

**5** If the needle point breaks off and no spare is available, it is possible to taper the broken end by rolling it under a finger against the abrasive side of a matchbox. While maintaining a continuous finger pressure, revolve the needle and slowly withdraw it from under the finger. Repeat this several times. In this way, some sort of point can be made, but it will never be as good as a new needle.

Having entered the needle into the tube or *needle spring box* (10), push it gently forward until the taper enters the nozzle at the front of the airbrush. Do not force it into the nozzle, but just let it touch, then tighten the *needle locking nut* (11), replace the *handle* (12) and make a trial spray with the *cam ring* (6) in the completely closed position. If adjusted correctly no colour should come from the airbrush when the finger button is forward and the air is allowed to flow. Test this by holding the airbrush, charged with diluted lamp black, close to a piece of paper and depressing the button, at the same time keeping it in its most forward position. Now, with the air flowing, move the finger button backwards and, if the needle and nozzle marry correctly, a fine spray should result. Should there be a spray when the cam ring is in the completely closed position, the needle must be released by the locking nut and repositioned.

Sometimes a gentle turn of the needle can assist with the adjustment. Tighten the needle locking nut again and make another trial. When the airbrush is operating correctly, it is possible to spray a line so thin as to be indistinguishable from a fine pencil line and to make a dot smaller than a pinhead. Most makes of airbrush have an adjustment so that the needle can be set to give a uniform volume of spray each time the air control is operated. This is used mostly by unskilled workers doing repetition colouring and is likely to cause a tiny blob at the commencement of each spray.

There are several systems of air and fluid control, the function of which is to regulate and balance the flow of air and colour.

Airflow is controlled by the downward and return movement of the *lever assembly* (5). When the lever is depressed the *air valve assembly* (17-23) is opened and the compressed air passes through the valve to the air cap. As the finger pressure is taken off the lever, the spring-loaded air valve closes, stopping the flow of compressed air.

Some manufacturers may not agree, but there are times when the ability to regulate the air flow with the finger is very useful. Some work, especially photographic retouching, calls for changing air flow and this is dealt with later under the heading 'How to use the airbrush', page 25.

Pressure can be regulated by various means. It is necessary to have a pump of some sort, or a container of compressed air, to create air pressure. This pressurised air must be contained in a holder or tank, preferably with a gauge, to ensure constant pressure without pulsations from the pump. The most satisfactory method of pressure control is to introduce a pressure regulator between tank and airbrush. With the aid of a regulator, the operator can select a working pressure which will remain constant.

**6**

**7**

**6** The working pressure range is usually a minimum of 18psi and a maximum of 35psi. Somewhere between 20psi and 30psi is suitable, but it very much depends on the type of work being done and the degree of atomisation required. A high pressure gives a fine atomisation and a smooth-looking result.

**7** Low pressure will result in a coarse or grainy surface and may cause blobs. Another factor which affects the appearance of the airbrushing is the distance the airbrush is held from the surface being sprayed. If the airbrush is held too far away, the spray can be coarse and possibly uneven, even though a high pressure is being used. If held closer it will be finer, but can be uneven on the work surface owing to inexperience. Like any other skill, that of airbrushing is only acquired by trial and error and practice.

Colour flow is regulated by the position of the *fluid needle* (13)—forwards for little colour flow and rearwards for a greater colour flow. As the needle moves backwards, the taper is withdrawn from the nozzle allowing the colour to flow more rapidly. The forward movement of the needle is assisted by a *needle spring* (9) housed in the *needle spring box* (10) at the rear of the body. When it moves forward, the taper on the needle reduces the colour flow. At the extreme of its forward movement, no colour is able to pass from the reservoir to the orifice of the nozzle. Never allow the finger control to fly forwards by suddenly releasing it—release it *gently*, otherwise damage may occur to the needle and nozzle.

In some makes of airbrush, the downward air control movement and the backward and forward colour control are linked. This may be an easy way of controlling both movements, but airbrush experts usually prefer independent control because with practice there is more flexibility. This is required especially by the photographic retoucher, who needs a very fine and changing balance between air and colour flow.

The *colour cup* or *reservoir* (14), holds the fluid or colour. A connecting tube allows the fluid to pass into the nozzle. In some types of airbrush the reservoir is part of the body as illustrated, but in others there is a removable reservoir so that the user can switch from one colour to another without waste or having to recharge the reservoir. With this latter removable reservoir method, a short spray away from the artwork should be given to clear the previous colour.

It is advisable to mix sufficient colour for the whole area in a palette before filling the reservoir, especially where a flat even area is required and matching is important. Some experts do a little mixing, to make a slight colour change, in the reservoir; when this is done, care should be taken to ensure that there are no lumps of colour on the mixing brush which could get into the tube connecting reservoir to nozzle and cause a blockage.

It is important to ensure that colour is free of small hardened lumps and that it is thoroughly mixed into its medium.

It is advisable to use colours in paste form from tubes or jars. Cakes of colour are not recommended, because not only is it possible to introduce small undissolved lumps of colour into the airbrush, but these cakes also tend to collect dust or even little pieces of eraser 'crumb'. It is important to replace caps on tubes and screw tops on jars in order to keep the contents dust- and lump-free.

This geometric design demonstrates the use of low tack film for masking different shapes. See page 39 for a full description of the stages in its preparation.

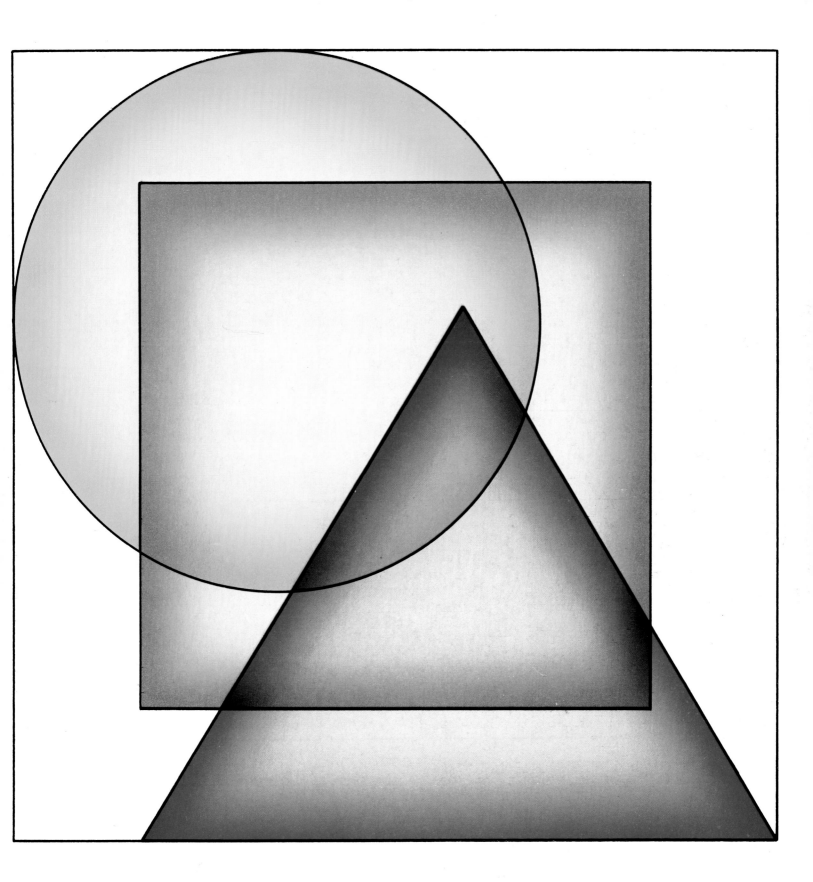

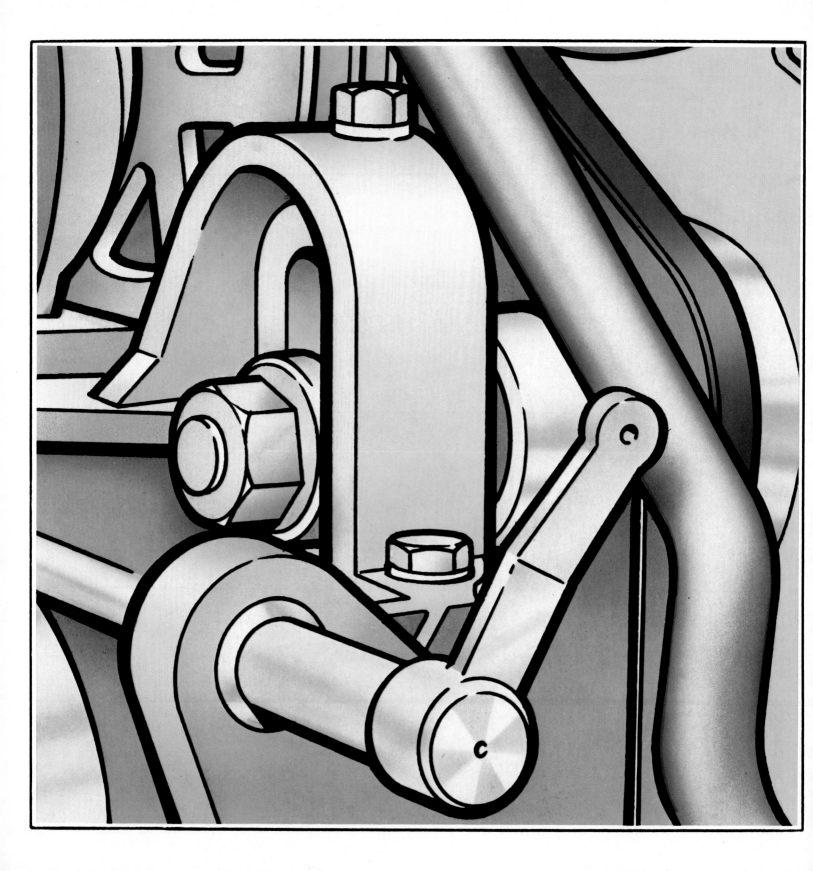

# Colour consistency

The colour to be sprayed should be of quite thin consistency, no thicker than milk. It is better to have it too watery than too thick. Thick colour through an airbrush will cause blobbing, poor flow and may even block the nozzle. Furthermore, thin or watery colour is easier for the beginner to control. It is advisable for the beginner to mix artists' quality lamp black and water to practise with. This will show different densities of grey according to the variation of the controls, and distance from airbrush to surface. It is important to use only colour which is finely ground if an airbrush is to be kept in top operating condition. Specially prepared retouching colours of varying degrees of grey are available as well as process black and white.

Poster colours should not be used because, owing to the coarse and abrasive nature of the pigment, they are liable to wear both the needle and the nozzle. Acrylic paint can be used, but should not be allowed to dry in the reservoir. If it does, soak or wash out with methylated spirits followed by water.

It cannot be stressed too strongly that the airbrush should be frequently cleaned, both during and after use. It is also advisable to spray through during use, and especially whenever the work is interrupted and when a job is completed.

Ink, both black and coloured, can be sprayed, but it is advisable to use non-waterproof inks as the waterproof type can dry quickly and clog the nozzle or harden in the reservoir. Should waterproof ink be used, it is

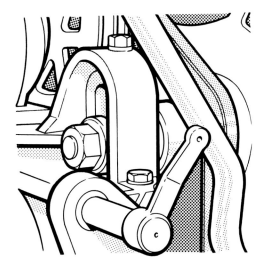

The artist is sometimes required to produce a piece of interesting pictorial artwork based on a dull technical subject. In this example the airbrush has been used to introduce colour and shape, resulting in an illustration which could well be used on the front cover to enhance an otherwise uninteresting or drab-looking publication.

advisable to wash the reservoir and the nozzle immediately with pen cleaner fluid. Incidentally, pen cleaner fluid can be used to dilute waterproof ink. It is useful to have two airbrushes—one for ink and the other for retouching or watercolour only. Dyes are also very suitable for use as they contain no particles of pigment.

After spraying artists' oil colour, the airbrush should be washed out and sprayed through with turpentine, followed by lighter fluid. Care should be taken not to allow any fluid to enter the slot through which the finger button protrudes.

A good quality round watercolour brush of about size No 6 is recommended for filling the reservoir with colour, water or cleaning fluid. It should be a brush in good condition and not some 'old faithful' which has started to moult. Stray hairs can get down into the nozzle and completely block the flow of colour and are difficult to remove (see 'Diagnosis of faults'). If colour has caked on to any part of the airbrush, a soft wooden toothpick may be used to loosen it.

On no account should dried colour be scratched out with divider points or similar sharp instruments. Scratching will leave tiny scores, making it all the easier for dried colour to adhere to the inner surface of the reservoir. If caking does occur, wash, wash and wash again with suitable medium, pen cleaner fluid or lighter fluid followed by water.

It is advisable while working to look occasionally at the front of the air cap, where colour can sometimes accumulate in the air cap guard. If not removed, a blob will be blown out on to the work surface. A blob of this nature indicates misalignment of air cap and nozzle.

If there is a small accumulation of colour, withdraw the needle with the finger button and clean the air cap with a small twist of damp cotton wool. It is imperative to withdraw the needle, otherwise the point will be bent.

When work is finished, examine the reservoir and air cap to make sure that no colour or ink has caked or dried. If left, such dried colour will eventually flake off, find its way into the nozzle and 'gum up the works' (see 'Diagnosis of faults').

**8**  To clear a blockage in the nozzle, dismantle the airbrush and very gently insert the fluid needle into the nozzle.

Watercolour airbrushing is very vulnerable to damage by untutored people putting their fingers on to the airbrushed area in order to indicate a particular feature. Another frequent cause of damage is by blowing off a piece of dust from the artwork; almost invariably a small spot of saliva is blown on to the work surface which, when dried, will leave a small ring.

Dust should be removed with a dust brush, a piece of cotton wool, lightly flicked off with a clean handkerchief or blown off with the air from an empty airbrush. Ensure that there are no small pieces of foreign matter adhering to the surface which is about to be airbrushed which will act as small masks preventing the colour from reaching the surface. Should this occur, do not attempt to cover the spots with further airbrushing; instead, carefully spot out the offending marks with the appropriate grey or colour on a small sable brush. When removing the airbrush from the airtube on completion of a piece of work, use the compressed air remaining in the air tank to blow any accumulation of dust and eraser crumbs off the desk.

# Air supply

The air supply must be of sufficient volume and pressure. The air should also be clean and dry. Equipment manufacturers supply literature which shows the various options ranging from small pressurised canisters and cylinders to foot pumps with compressed-air receiver tanks and on to larger electric-motor-driven air compressors with receiving tanks as a complete unit.

Because of cost, it may be necessary for the would-be airbrush artist to begin with a foot pump unit, but my advice would be to graduate as quickly as funds will allow to an electrically driven unit. Using a foot pump can be frustrating; just as the airbrush is working nicely at the correct pressure, the pressure can drop and it is necessary to do some more pumping before the cycle begins all over again.

An alternative is to use a car tyre on its wheel. This can be inflated at a service station and be taken into the studio to be used as a very effective and economical compressed air supply, although the valve and air hose connector need to be adapted in order to obtain an airtight connection.

In studios where airbrushes are extensively used, the usual practice is to install an electrically driven unit, with automatic cut off, near the studio, but preferably outside to remove the irritating noise. From the air receiver tank a pipe is run into the studio and then round the wall to each artist's work point. This main pipe should be galvanised, copper or PVC because of the water content in the air, and should occasionally be blown through with compressed air to remove any accumulation of water. At each work point a secondary line is run from the main air line to the most convenient position to suit each artist. Here a small air pressure regulating valve can be fitted, so that the artist can select his own working pressure.

The author uses an adapted motor and pump from an old refrigerator, which has been giving good service for the last twenty years.

It is advisable to introduce some sort of moisture trap so that condensed moisture in the air system does not find its way through to the airbrush. The air tank itself acts as a moisture trap and should be drained periodically. A drain plug is usually fitted at the lower part of the tank.

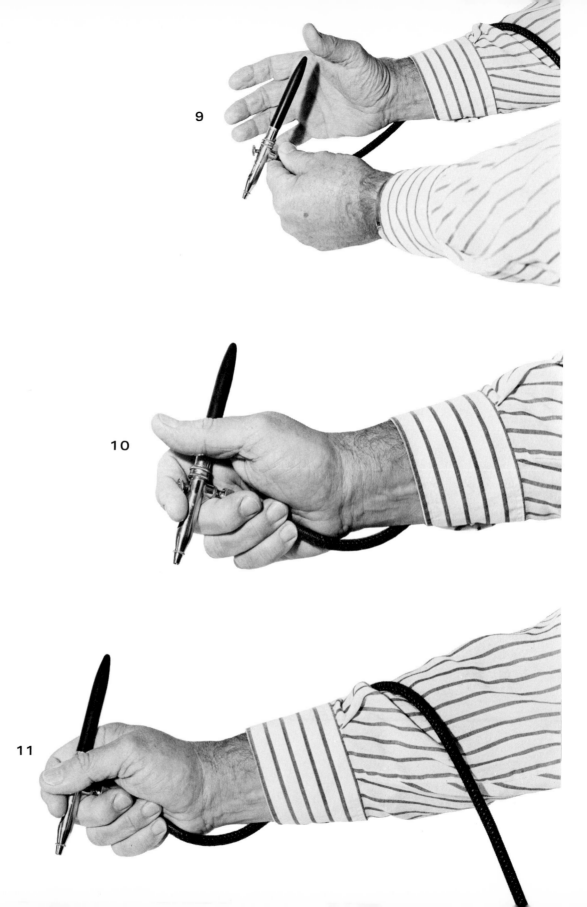

# How to use the airbrush

Like any other instrument or tool, it is necessary to hold the airbrush properly to obtain the best results.

The air hose should be routed from below and not trailing over the top of the desk on which work is being done. It should be of sufficient length to allow free movement of the arm.

**9** Holding the airbrush in the left hand, assuming the user is righthanded, move the right arm clockwise over to the right of the air hose, then left under it, so that the hose wraps itself around the forearm and wrist. Transfer the airbrush to the right hand and hold it like a pen, with the fourth and little fingers holding the air hose and air valve box. In this manner, the air hose is kept off the desk and working surface and cannot knock over water jars, pots of paint and cups of tea. In general, the airbrush should be operated at an angle of between 75° and 80° to the work surface, but this may vary according to the work being done. Now, with the filling brush, charge the reservoir with diluted lamp black and make sure that the air supply is at a working pressure. Next comes the all-important operation of the air/colour control lever assembly.

**10** The way to get positive operation is to place the forefinger on the flat top of the control so that it rests on the joint between the first and second segments of the finger. The finger tip will, in fact, if the brush is held correctly, be resting on the left side of the body of the airbrush, over the lip of the reservoir.

**11** Now place the thumb on the forefinger so that both forefinger and thumb are in contact with the control and the air hose is lying in a natural position under the other fingers. The third finger is under the body of the airbrush, partly holding the air hose and partly holding the air valve box.

This method of holding the airbrush does not apply to those instruments with a large 'cup' type reservoir. With such instruments, it is not possible to hold it in the recommended way, nor is it necessary because they are intended mainly for spraying large areas for which the 'stand back and squirt' method is acceptable. Finer work requires the smaller type of instrument calling for a more competent operator. With the lever assembly control in the extreme forward position, depress it to allow air to pass into the body of the airbrush and out through the air cap. Do not try to depress the control with the forefinger alone. Instead, tighten the hand so as to give the airbrush a squeeze. It will probably be found that as this is done, air will flow, but if not, just give a little extra pressure with the forefinger. This combination of squeeze and forefinger pressure will give you control over how much air is allowed to enter the airbrush.

Holding the airbrush in this way may at first feel awkward but if, after a little practice, you try using the tip of the forefinger alone, you will find it will give less control than the method recommended. An appreciation of the value of being able to control the air flow will develop as more experience is gained in the use of the airbrush.

Next we come to the control of the flow of colour. This is quite easy if

**12**

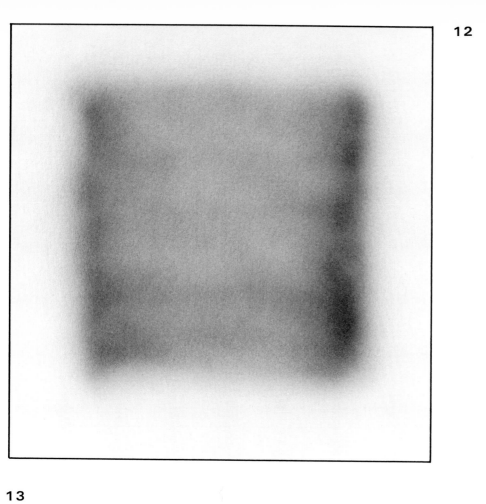

**13**

**14**

the airbrush is held as described, because while pressing to regulate the air flow, the lever assembly is also eased slightly to the rear with the forefinger and thumb. This withdraws the taper of the needle from the nozzle, the colour is drawn through the orifice of the air cap by the passage of air, is atomised and then sprayed on to the work surface.

Experimentation with different combinations of air pressure, air flow and colour flow will give a wide range of effects; at the same time experience will be gained of the control positions required and how to achieve a definite, planned result and not just a 'squirt and hope for the best'. The operator will be in charge—not the airbrush.

# Practice exercises

The airbrush is not an easy instrument to handle if fine and accurate work is required; it is simply not possible to become an expert after a few trial 'squirts'. The following exercises using lamp black watercolour and clean water will give useful experience.

**12** With a pencil, draw a rough area about 15.5cm (6in) square and airbrush a flat grey area. Try to keep to the shape, although it does not matter if the spray goes beyond the pencil lines. Move the airbrush right and left, gradually working down from top to bottom of the square. The grey area here is uneven because the operator did not stop the flow of air and colour as he changed direction.

**13** Try to get an even tone over the whole area by momentarily stopping the spray at each change of direction. Provided that the needle is not pulled back too far, it can maintain the same position while the air is halted at the end of each stroke. This 'on and off' operation will also increase general control of the airbrush. Further practice may be gained by 'correcting' uneven efforts by applying little puffs of colour to the lighter patches to achieve uniformity.

**14** Repeat the exercise above, except that the top of the square should be light grey, toning progressively darker to nearly black at the bottom. This exercise can be repeated in reverse.

**15**

**16**

**17**

**15** Draw two straight vertical pencil lines about 10cm (4in) apart; starting at top on the lefthand line, airbrush a series of thin horizontal lines stopping on the righthand line. These lines should not have thicker or denser blobs at each end. This is probably one of the most difficult skills to acquire, but a competent operator should be able to airbrush lines as thin as a pencil line and without blobs. Some manufacturers recommend complicated manoeuvres to avoid blobs, but if skill is acquired in controlling the on/off air movement and provided that the brush is operating efficiently, there should be no blob. A small dot of colour may occur if the lever assembly is pulled back too far because the needle has opened up a larger passage in the nozzle, allowing the colour to flow and accumulate in a small droplet at the orifice of the nozzle. To avoid this either do not pull the needle back too far or, if you do, first give a little spray away from the job before starting. In fact it is always best to do a little test spray on a spare piece of paper.

**16** Sample of a brush ruling practice exercise (see below).

**17** Repeat the previous exercise but with the airbrush resting against a steel rule—known as brush ruling. Rest the edge of the rule on the work surface and support it at an angle of about 30° by putting all the fingers of one hand under it. Place the thumb partly on the upper side of the rule and partly on the working surface. Now rest the knurled ring of the aircap on the upper edge of the rule and slide the airbrush left and right to get the feel of it. Then, guided by the rule, airbrush straight lines without blobs at each end. The finger positions may be varied a little in order to find those which are the most comfortable. The thickness of line can be varied according to the angle of the rule which regulates the distance from airbrush to working surface.

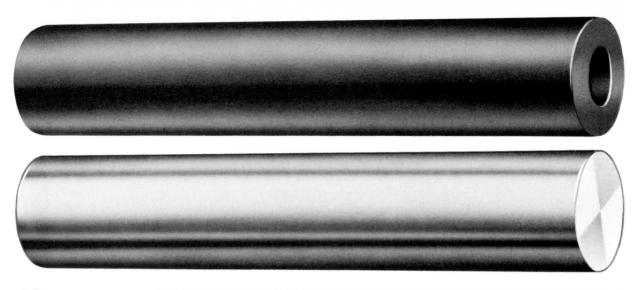

18

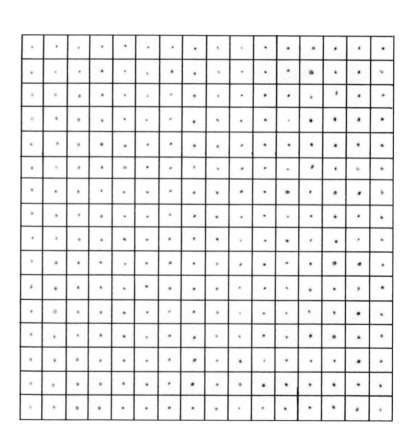

19

**18** Two effective examples of finished brush ruling. The rollers in retouched Illustration 40 have been airbrushed in this way. This exercise can be repeated using process white on black or dark-grey paper or a bromide print to develop the ability to airbrush highlights along edges; the highlights can be finished off by brush ruling solid white along the centre to give more emphasis.

**19** With the nozzle of the airbrush approximately 0.5cm ($\frac{1}{4}$in) from the work surface, spray small dots. The first efforts will probably look like spiders with big feet, but keep trying! Use varying distances from the work surface, for this is where the ability to control air and colour flow will become apparent. This exercise not only increases operating control but develops the ability to airbrush quite small highlights. Then draw a grid, like graph paper, with squares of about 0.5cm ($\frac{1}{4}$in) and make an airbrush dot in the centre of each square. This develops the ability to direct the colour precisely where it is required.

Practise airbrushing curved lines to develop the ability to airbrush shapes with soft edges and curved highlights (see Illustrations 32, 33, 34 and 35).

At no time should the fingers actually come into contact with the paper, board or photograph being worked on. Always use a hand sheet to prevent hand grease getting on to the work surface (see Illustration 47). This applies not only to airbrushing, but also to any work where the hand is rested on the work surface.

# Masking shapes

Very frequently it is necessary to airbrush a precise shape, with clean sharp edges. This is done by cutting a mask or stencil. A very simple mask is a piece of flat material such as cartridge paper with the desired shape cut out of it. This is placed in position on the work surface and held down with fingers or weights—several coins are quite effective. The disadvantage of this type of mask is that colour is liable to creep under the edges as the air lifts them, especially if a high air pressure is used. With all the following methods, a trial should first be made on a spare piece of the same work surface to ensure that the surface will not be damaged when the mask is lifted.

**20** To mask a shape with straight edges, or even one straight edge which is part of the drawing, masking tape can be laid down outside the area. To extend the masked area, cut pieces of paper to go under the outer edges of the tape. This photograph shows the shape being prepared for Illustration 6.

**21** Retouchers use cleanly cut pieces of paper for airbrushing one or two straight edges. These usually are held down with the fingers, weights or with a steel rule and fingers. A friendly printer will cut scrap paper for this purpose and the size most retouchers like is about 23cm (9in) long and 6.5cm ($2\frac{1}{2}$in) wide. Coated paper is best, because the edge does not cockle as quickly when it becomes damp. Paper can also be cut with curved edges and used as described above.

A series of different sized circles is very useful, especially if cut from clear, stiff celluloid or acetate. These can be cut with sharp-pointed dividers. Place one point in the centre and score the circle deeply with the other point, remove the dividers and bend the celluloid on the score mark so that the circle breaks away. With a little practice, a sharp, clean edge can be obtained. Keep both the inner and outer portions as both will be useful at various times.

This pattern demonstrates how very simple airbrushing can produce an effective result. The outer area was masked with tape and paper and diagonal guide lines were marked on the masking paper. Using a thin piece of card as a mask and following the guide lines, green watercolour was sprayed, followed by yellow. The card was simply held in place by finger pressure.

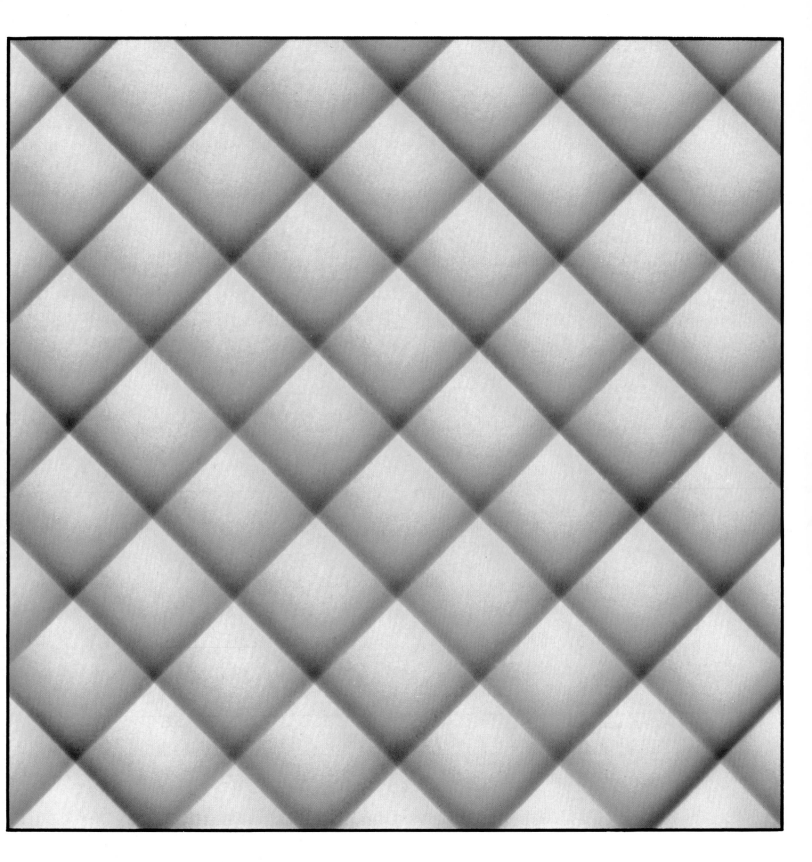

This effect was obtained by folding a piece of cartridge paper into a concertina shape. The extreme edges of the 'valleys' were held in place by pins to prevent any movement during spraying. A spray of sepia was airbrushed from one direction at a low angle, and a spray of orange from the reverse direction. The secondary lines of airbrushing halfway between each orange and sepia spray came about as 'accidentals'; during the spraying of the main colours, some colour bounced back on to the facing surface causing this interesting effect. The paper was then ironed flat and mounted on card.

**22**  A soft edge can be achieved by using a piece of cardboard to make the mask; an even softer edge can be obtained by putting another piece of cardboard under the mask, to raise it further from the work surface. This allows some of the colour to find its way under the mask, thus retaining the shape but not a clearly defined edge.

**23**  To mask complicated shapes with sharp, clean edges it is necessary to use a mask which adheres to the work surface. Self-adhesive low tack plastic sheet makes life easy for the airbrush artist and can be laid on almost any surface. Large pieces can be saved and used again. Illustration 23 shows one of the stages in the preparation of the colour illustration on page 17, which demonstrates how one piece of low tack film can be used for three different colour sprays. Having drawn the outlines in ink for clarity, the whole design was covered with low tack film which extended beyond the outer square by about 2.5cm (1in). Beyond that, the surface was further masked by slipping pieces of straight-edged paper, about 7cm (2¾in) wide, under the outer edges of the film. In this way the film was used economically and the surrounding surface completely covered.

The spray sequence was as follows:
1   The yellow circle was cut and the inner film lifted. Yellow ink was then airbrushed, but in order to keep the centre as white as possible, the airbrush was directed outwards from the centre of the circle.
2   Having made sure that the yellow ink was dry, the circle of low tack film was replaced. Next the triangle was cut out and sprayed as above.
3   When the blue ink was dry and the triangle of film replaced, the square was cut out and sprayed. The outer masking film and surrounding paper were then removed.

This demonstrates how simple the masking procedure can be if the cutting sequence is pre-determined, although in this particular case masking and spraying could have been in any order. Ink was used because of its transparency in order to achieve the interesting tones when the colours are superimposed.

To avoid making a pinhole at the centre of a circle, draw two crossed short lines intersecting at right angles. With rubber gum, mount a small piece of card on the lines so that the ends are visible and will act as a guide to transfer the lines on to the card. Stick the point of the compass or dividers into the intersection, draw the circle and then remove the mounted card.

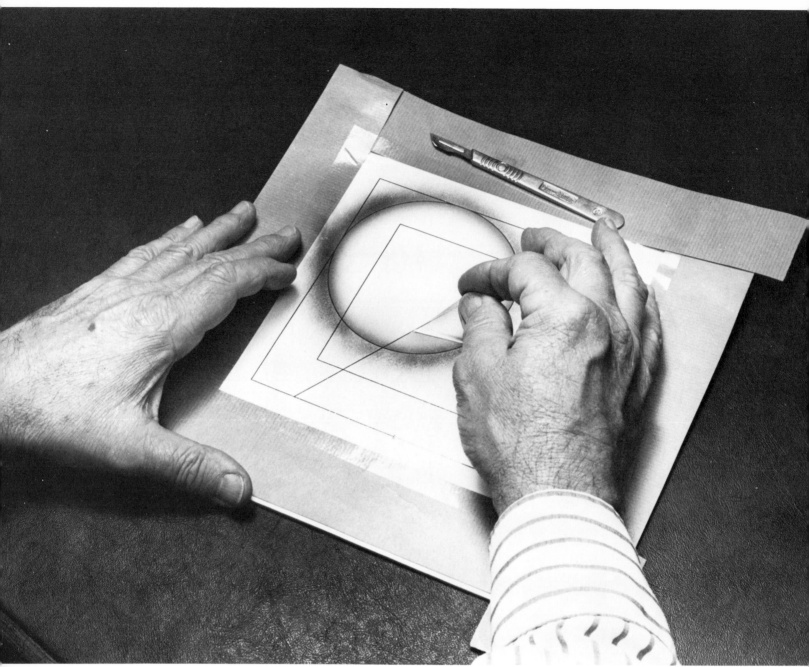

As an alternative to using low tack plastic sheet, rubber gum and tracing paper can be used as in the colour illustration on page 64. Draw the shape on the work surface in pencil or ink, or in colour if the defining edge is to be part of the design, and spread rubber gum thinly over the line about 2.5cm (1in) wide. If there are several small shapes, cover the whole area and then, while the rubber gum is still tacky, spread a piece of tracing paper over the whole area. If prolonged airbrushing is necessary, it is as well to gum both the work surface and the tracing paper. Allow almost to dry. Lay down the tracing paper over the work area and burnish with something smooth and flat. With a sharp blade—a pointed surgical scalpel is ideal—cut through the tracing paper along the line of the shape, which can be . seen through it. Try not to cut deeper than the thickness of the tracing paper. Having cut all round the shape, lift the middle and allow the exposed gum to dry. When it is dry, remove with a 'bungee'—that is a lump of hardened rubber solution. To make a bungee spread some gum on a flat glazed surface, allow to dry for a few hours, and then roll up into a ball. This can be used like an eraser and will lift the film of dried gum from the work surface. Make sure that all the gum is removed, especially at the edges of the mask, to ensure a crisp edge when airbrushing is complete. Having airbrushed the shape, lift the mask and remove the remaining gum with the bungee.

Incidentally, it is wise to keep the piece of mask you have lifted in case you wish to airbrush round the outside of the shape already sprayed. After the colour is dry, replace the centre part to fit exactly into its hole and then lift the outer part. But do test first to ensure that no damage will be caused to the surface. If a mask is to be cut so that an airbrushed area is to be covered with masking material, it is important to ensure that the sprayed part does not get damaged. It is possible to protect by spraying with diluted clear gum arabic, but make sure the airbrush is thoroughly washed with clean water afterwards as gum arabic can go very hard when dry, causing blockage. Alternatively, some of the modern aerosol film sprays are suitable, but test before using because of possible colour or density change.

When a considerable amount of airbrushing is necessary, such as obliterating backgrounds or other details on photographs, it is not advisable to attempt to complete the work in one go. It is better to apply one spray, allow it to dry, and then give another application, and continue in this manner until the desired effect has been attained.

When extensive spraying is done, especially if process white is mixed into colour, a powdery surface may result. This sort of surface is very vulnerable, is easily scratched and will lift in uneven patches if masking material is laid on it in order to cut a mask for an adjacent shape. The remedy is to take a piece of cotton wool and, keeping it in a fluffy state, gently wipe over the sprayed surface to remove the powdery finish. Do not allow the cotton wool to become hard or scratching will occur. Having removed the soft powdery surface, a masking material may be laid over the sprayed surface with far less risk of damage. A light spray of diluted gum arabic will make the surface even more secure, but make sure it is thoroughly dry before further masking.

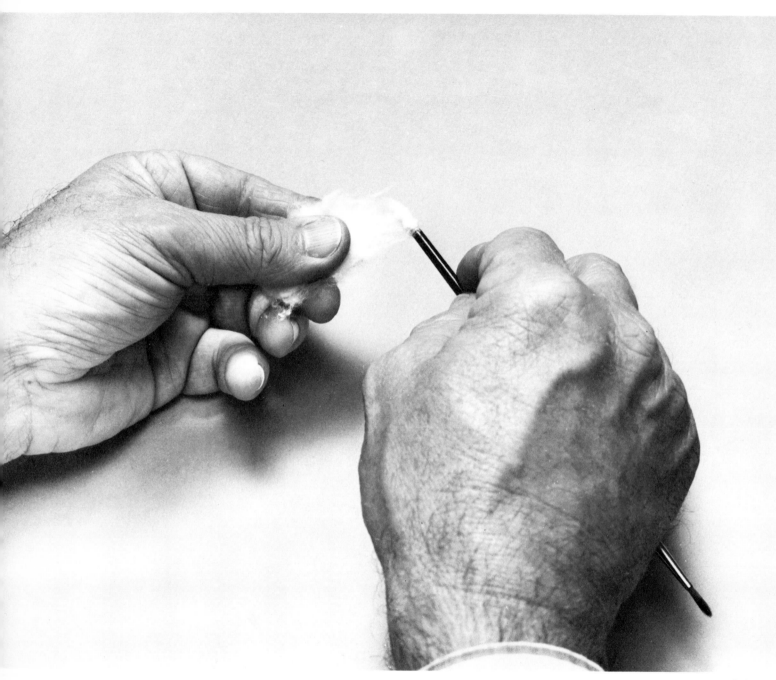

**24** Because it is possible to wash airbrushing from the surface of a photoprint, it is often not necessary to cut a mask; instead the chosen area can be airbrushed so that the spray goes beyond the final shape. The surplus spray can then be removed, leaving the required shape. A watercolour brush is sharpened off at the end and, with this pointed end dampened with the tongue, a small piece of cotton wool is attached by twirling the brush. Now dampen the cotton wool (you can't beat spit) and wipe off the unwanted spray. By this method, quite small areas can be removed and clean edges obtained.

Masking fluid can be used when it is necessary to mask a small area or to cover a small patch, such as a bolt head or nut. Several commercial products with a latex base are available. A little blob of rubber gum thinned out with lighter fluid and applied with a small brush works quite well, but be sure to wash out the brush with more lighter fluid.

Cheap but effective masking fluid can be 'home-made' in the following way. Take one egg, break the shell and pour the yolk and white into the cupped hands. Hold under gently running cold water (not hot otherwise the egg will cook) and, by passing the egg from one hand to the other, wash away the white without breaking the yolk. When all the white is washed away, hold the yolk in one cupped hand and, with the thumb and forefinger of the other hand, pinch the skin of the yolk to break it, whilst simultaneously allowing the yolk, minus skin, to drop into a small clean screwtop jar. Then into the yolk mix a quarter of a teaspoonful of borax and a little process white. The borax prevents the yolk from going bad, and the process white provides a little pigment, so that you can see where you are applying the egg. Now paint this mixture on to the surface to be masked, adding a little water if it is too thick. This mixture will last for months, but do not let it dry out in the jar. Having painted it on the area of photoprint to be masked, allow it to dry and then airbrush as desired. When the sprayed colour has dried, gently scrape off the egg with a suitable piece of wood such as the end of a brush cut to a wedge shape, but be careful not to damage the print or paper surface.

Remove the scraped-off crumbs of egg with a dust brush as quickly as possible, because otherwise a grease deposit will be left on the airbrushed area and cause a darkening effect. If such a deposit occurs, wipe over with a lighter fluid on cotton wool to remove it.

If the previously 'egged' area is to be sprayed, wipe it over with lighter fluid on cotton wool in order to remove the slight grease deposit which, like fingerprints, will repel sprayed colour, causing it to become 'blobby'. Alternatively, mix ox gall into the water colour to be sprayed, but don't get any on the tongue—it tastes foul!

**25**

**25** An interesting cloud effect can be achieved by masking with cotton wool. First the outer area was masked and then pieces of cotton wool were pulled into ragged shapes. These were then stuck down in the required positions with rubber gum. The background was then sprayed an overall light grey followed by darker shading in places. While spraying is taking place, the edges of the cotton wool blow in various directions creating a soft edge. Having completed the spraying, the cotton wool was lifted and the rubber gum removed. Next the shadows were airbrushed to give form and substance to the cloud. Finally highlights were introduced with a glass eraser.

Much of the airbrushing undertaken by an artist may be more complex than the mere spraying of a flat or gradated tone in a single shape. The artwork may require multiple sprays and it is probable that no two pieces of work will have the same approach. For this reason, it is not possible to lay down hard and fast recommendations regarding the order in which various colours or shapes should be airbrushed. Take a good long look at the structure of the drawing and work out the steps to be taken and the order in which masks are to be cut. The artist should not look upon his work as a series of disconnected airbrushed shapes, but should visualise the finished result as a whole and then work towards this end. By so doing, very often a simpler order of work may be arrived at. For instance, having cut a mask to a shape, a spray of one colour followed by a spray of another colour over part of the area may achieve an effect much more easily and satisfactorily than by separate spraying with a different mask.

Again, it is possible to take short cuts by cutting masks for two adjacent areas from one sheet of masking paper or film. One of the areas can be exposed and sprayed, then the adjoining area exposed and sprayed (see Illustration 23 and colour illustration on page 17). In this way some of the second spray may be allowed to superimpose on the first, thus changing its density or colour characteristic. With the use of a loose piece of paper cut to a shape and laid down with fingers or weights, a third shape may be obtained. It will quickly be seen that, whilst the principle of masking is very simple, the multiplicity of uses presents many possibilities to achieve design and effect.

The artist can also save himself time and work if he determines which of the shapes in his design are to be of the same colour. By cutting several shapes in various parts of his design, he can spray the chosen colour even though they may be of various densities. Although only one colour is sprayed at a time, a combination of sprays will bring about an infinite variety of results. The artist should also not lose sight of the basic principles of drawing, highlights, shadows and reflected secondary highlights—in fact, those factors which go to make shape, contour, solidity, atmosphere, character and realism, all of which contribute to the creation of a piece of artwork, commercial or otherwise.

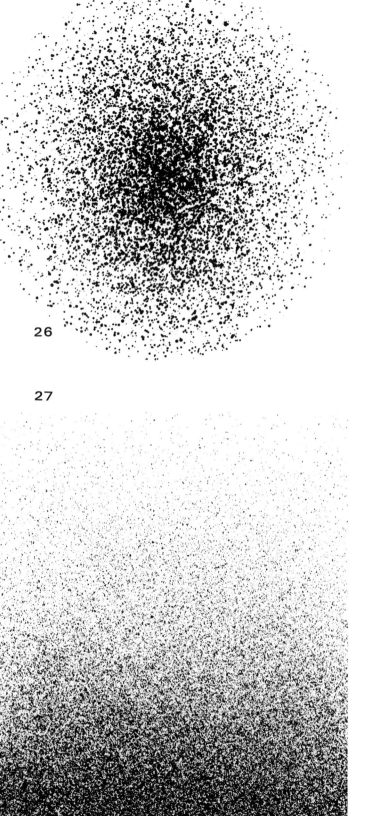

26

27

28

# Splatter

This most versatile effect is obtained either by removing the air cap on airbrushes with a fixed or screwed-in nozzle, or by replacing the aircap with a splatter cap. The splatter effect occurs because the colour is not finely atomised, but instead emerges in blobs. The size of the blobs can be altered by varying the air pressure and by varying the colour flow.

**26** A low pressure will cause large blobs, especially when the needle is drawn back to allow a free flow of colour. Here black ink has been used at low pressure.

**27** Finer splatter is obtained if more air pressure is used, and here again the size of the blobs is affected by colour flow. The air pressure used for this example was 22psi. A little experimentation will soon reveal the variety of effects that can be obtained.

One of the advantages of splatter is that when black is sprayed it can be reproduced 'line', ie a line block can be made for letterpress printing. In this way, a line drawing can be shaded with splatter in the same way that screen tints are used.

**28** Interesting textures are possible not only when spraying black, but with various greys. This example shows how a rough effect may be obtained with a combination of smooth spray, which was first graduated from a mid tone at the top down to white at the bottom. Then white was splattered on this smooth tone, with a greater concentration at the top. Next a dark grey was splattered from the bottom graduating upwards. A realistic concrete effect can be achieved on an illustration of a building in this way using a mixture of splatters on the same surface. The splatter does not have to be an all-over flat tone, but can be shaded with splatter or, by replacing the aircap, shading with finely atomised colour.

When colours, especially bright ones, are splattered either on their own or in combination, the effect is most rewarding and will lead the illustrator to some very satisfactory effects (see colour illustration on page 54). Unusual backgrounds can also be produced with splatter for use in conjunction with other artwork. Additionally, a splattered background can be prepared on card, or white or coloured paper, to be used in photographic work.

Sometimes a retoucher is required to work on a 'grainy' photograph; if finely atomised airbrushing is done, it usually looks false because the sprayed surface does not marry in with the rest of the print, but fine splatter can often achieve a good match. Try some splatter, because, in my opinion, it is a much-neglected technique.

# Special effects

A great variety of effects can be obtained from airbrushing. These can be used to introduce texture, to produce an interesting background for an advertisement, or as a background on which to photograph jewellery, engineering components and so on. An imaginative artist or photographer will soon recognise the infinite possibilities once the principle is understood. Some suggestions for effects to try are given below.

**29** Crush a piece of paper into a ball, straighten it out so that it lies fairly, but not completely, flat. Spray from one side at a low level. The spray will touch one side only of each little hillock, thus exaggerating the effect of light and shade. Now mount the sprayed paper as flat as possible. A most interesting effect can be obtained by using the same 'crumpled paper' idea, but with one colour sprayed from one direction and another colour sprayed from the opposite direction (see dust jacket). Next slightly dampen the back of the paper and smooth out with a not-too-hot electric iron. The sheet can then be mounted on card with paste or rubber gum; dry-mounting with tissue and hot press is even better as the paper is made quite flat by this method.

A quite different effect from a similar technique is created by concertina-folding a piece of cartridge paper and again spraying different colours from different directions (see colour illustration on page 36).

Cut a series of shapes—simplified animals, cars, sports equipment, aeroplanes, etc. Lay them on the work surface—touching, overlapping, symmetrical, haphazard—and spray flat or shaded tones (see colour illustration on page 53).

Take small objects—finger rings, crown stoppers, buttons, blobs of cotton wool, coins, leaves, etc—the list is endless. Spray directly from above or from an angle.

Weight down a d'oyley and spray through the holes. Individual Valentine cards, birthday cards, etc can be made in this way.

Yet another interesting effect is shown in the colour illustration on page 35.

**30**

## Repetitive airbrushing

Work of a repetitive nature such as colouring on short runs, spraying designs on to models, ceramics, maps, plans, toys, lampshades, fabrics, signs and so on, does not demand a high degree of skill from the operator. For such work, it would be uneconomical to cut a separate mask for each object to be sprayed, so a stencil should be prepared. A special stencil paper is available from suppliers of artists' materials; this resists impregnation and therefore does not cockle round the cut edges.

An imitation vellum or parchment used for lampshade making is ideal for making durable stencils. Alternatively, a satisfactory waterproof stencil can be made by rubbing paraffin wax (candle grease), on to a piece of fairly thick paper and then cutting the desired shape. Another method is to draw the required shape or design on a piece of thick drawing paper and coat both sides of the paper with shellac; when dry, cut out the shape and airbrush as required. It is useful to cut more than one stencil so that one can dry whilst the other is being used.

When doing this sort of airbrushing, hold the airbrush at right angles to the work surface to prevent the colour from creeping under the edges of the stencil. When using stencils which are not stuck down, but merely laid on the work, it is advisable to use as low a pressure as possible to avoid the stencil or mask from lifting. It is also good practice to spray away from the edge where possible, as this will also prevent lifting.

When inexperienced operators are using the airbrush, the cam ring or needle adjusting screw should be set so that the operator has only to depress the finger button in order to spray the colour.

## Photographic retouching

Photographic retouching can best be learned by practical tuition from an expert, but retouching techniques have been included here because the airbrush is one of the instruments extensively used by the retoucher. The word 'retouching' is applied to work done on both negatives and photoprints.

Co-operation between the photographer and retoucher before the photograph is taken can save time and work later. Any features which would otherwise have to be removed on the print could be eliminated at an early stage, but unfortunately it is rare for the retoucher to have any say in the photography. For example, if the subject of the photograph is car tyres, they will often be dirty, having been rolled along the floor. If, before the photographs are taken, the tyres are first washed and, when dry, the name of the manufacturer on the wall of the tyre emphasised by an application of chalk, this would save a great deal of retouching.

**30** Highly polished subjects can also be treated prior to photography with an airbrush by first spraying them with milk to reduce and soften the reflections, so that subsequent retouching is kept to a minimum. Quite

The shapes of a variety of transport subjects were traced on to cartridge paper and cut out. The square was drawn in black ink on card and masked with tape and paper around its outer edges. Rubber solution was spread on both card and mask, and the mask was mounted in position on the card. The dried rubber solution was removed from the 'holes' with a bungee and the exposed areas airbrushed with blue ink—ink being used because of its transparency. When dry, the mask was lifted and the remaining adhesive cleaned off. The surface and mask were then again covered with rubber solution, this time using the mask in reverse, and the mask was again mounted in position. Surplus adhesive was removed before green ink was airbrushed over the whole area. When dry, the masks were lifted and the rubber solution removed.

To achieve this coarse splatter, the airbrush was used at low pressure and, to vary the size of the very coarse blobs, the finger button was moved backwards and forwards.

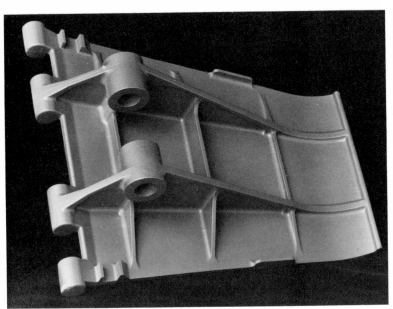

**31**

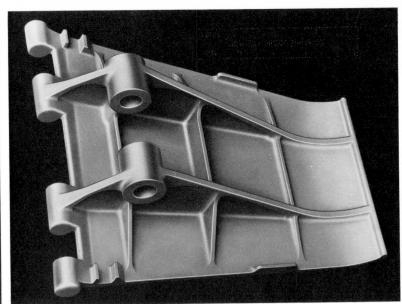

**32**

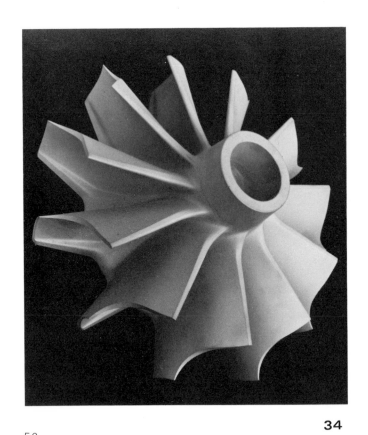

**34**

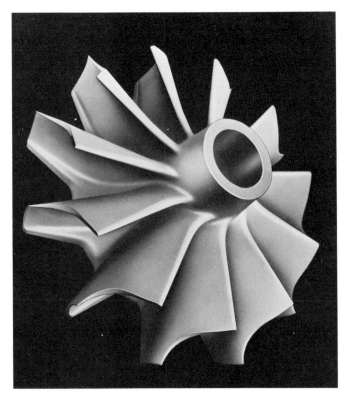

**33**

often, no further airbrushing is required on the actual print; some judicious handwork will produce a very satisfactory and more natural looking result. The silver goblet on the right in this illustration was sprayed with milk prior to taking the photograph; there has been no subsequent retouching.

Aerosol sprays containing a white fluid are available with which to spray silver and other highly polished subjects, but because the atomisation is inferior to the airbrush, the subject usually takes on a chalky appearance and, if over-done, can cause the surface of the article to appear to have been sand-blasted. My recommendation is to airbrush milk or, as a good substitute, process white.

**31-36** Three pairs of photographs before and after retouching showing how surfaces and highlights have been airbrushed. Additional handwork was done to strengthen highlights, shadows and details.

**35**

**36**

**37**

**38**

**37 & 38**  Airbrushing is often used in photo retouching to subdue rather than to obliterate detail. In this case, the handmade furniture was really the subject of the photograph, not the carpet, which caused confusion and tended to dominate because of its pattern. First the outer edge of the photograph and the furniture were masked with low tack film and cut so that the carpet could be sprayed. A mid-tone grey, mixed with lamp black, process white and a little sepia, was sprayed over the carpet. Because of its constituents, the mid-tone grey made the dark part of the carpet lighter and the light part darker. Some shadows were then airbrushed with lamp black. The masks were lifted and handwork completed the retouching, with no further airbrush work. Very often there is a temptation to airbrush reflections or to smooth out surfaces, but where possible it is far better to use natural reflections, as on the table top. Airbrushing should not be obvious. The biggest compliment that can be paid to a retoucher, after having done several hours' work, is to be told that his work cannot be detected.

40

## 39 & 40

These two 'before and after' photographs show how the airbrush is used to completely remove unsightly detail. First the outer edges, the car, the free standing console with gauges and the roller bed were masked, leaving the floor and white sheeting exposed. The line where floor and wall were to meet was marked on the outer masking paper and a first spray of process white was airbrushed over the floor and future wall. Using the guide line of wall and floor junction, the wall area was covered with a straight-edged piece of paper and held down with a steel rule and weights. The floor was then sprayed with a mid-grey. Next dark-grey splatter and white splatter (see Illustration 28) was applied. The next stage was to cover the floor with straight-edged paper, rule and weights and airbrush the wall with an off-white. The tile effect was then obtained by simply ruling pencil lines on the off-white airbrushing.

The next step was to cut the masking film to uncover the rollers. These were cleaned up with mid-grey followed by highlights and darks, which were brush ruled with the airbrush to give a cylindrical effect. This is an example of how useful the ability to brush rule is. Finally, a few shadows were airbrushed, the cord replaced, the film lifted and, with a little handwork on the car and the small instrument, the job was completed.

This sunrise cloud effect was achieved by spreading rubber gum on the masked area and, when dry, partially removing it. A circular mask was positioned for the sun. The area was then airbrushed in various colours and, when dry, removed with a bungee. Finally, the clouds were softened with a glass brush and a little colour was sprayed over the sun to give a misty effect.

This stylised landscape emphasises the versatility of the airbrush, once the skill of spraying gradated tone has been acquired. The sequence of airbrushing operations used was as follows:

The lines of the hills and contours were drawn in pencil on card and then the whole area was covered with rubber solution adhesive and tracing paper. The sky area was cut, following the outline of the hills seen through the tracing paper; the tracing paper removed was retained for use later. After removing the dried rubber solution, tracing paper was torn into the main shapes of the clouds—two large shapes and four smaller shapes. These were then mounted in position with rubber adhesive, some of which was allowed to extend beyond the cloud area. When dry, the adhesive was partially removed by dragging a bungee in a horizontal direction in order to leave some of the adhesive on the surface. The artist has an idea of what is required, but there is an element of luck about achieving satisfactory 'accidentals'. In this case, after the sky was airbrushed and the tracing paper and adhesive removed, an acceptable cloud effect appeared. The sky and light area of water were airbrushed with ink to achieve luminosity, but the remainder of the water and the hills were airbrushed with watercolour for density.

Before proceeding to the next operation, the sky was fixed by spraying with diluted gum arabic; in fact, each area was fixed immediately after the colour was sprayed in order to protect the airbrushed surface. The piece of tracing paper which had been cut from the sky area was then replaced, using rubber adhesive on both the tracing paper and the airbrushed surface. Having been cut from the sky area, the paper fitted exactly. The hill, water and foreground areas were airbrushed separately, the masking of each area being removed and replaced as and when necessary, and the airbrushed section fixed immediately after each spraying.

If it is found that the tracing paper shapes become a little difficult to handle, a fresh paper mask may be cut, but it is important to ensure that the dark areas slightly overlap the light to avoid any white gaps. For this reason, it is advisable to airbrush the light areas first. The very dark hills and their reflection in the water were cut as one mask. After airbrushing the gradated tone of the reflection, a piece of card was laid along the distant shoreline and the hill itself airbrushed to the darker tone.

Some handwork was carried out to give the impression of trees, to break up the hard line, and to make good any little white gaps which might have occurred. The clouds were given a little texture by using the torn edge of the original cloud shape as a mask and finally the light reflections on the water and shoreline were brush ruled with white and grey.

**41**

**41 & 42** Another example of how the airbrush is used in photo retouching to remove unwanted detail and for improving surfaces. Although considerable airbrushing was undertaken, a natural appearance has been retained by leaving the ground untouched. In this sort of work the main source of light should be noted, so that airbrushed highlights are positioned correctly, including secondary highlights. Apart from the airbrushing, extensive handwork was done to emphasise detail and give a bright crisp appearance.

42

# Negative retouching

Modern photographers rarely use negative sizes above 5in x 4in and a great deal of work is done on a $2\frac{1}{4}$in x $2\frac{1}{4}$in format. These sizes make it impractical to do extensive work on the negative but, to remove completely a portion of the image, a special preparation can be painted on to the emulsion side. This is called photopaque, stopping out medium or liquid opaque. A vignette effect is achieved by spraying photopaque around the outer edge of the negative, thus preventing light from being transmitted, which in turn results in a white area when the positive photoprint is developed. Another way to achieve this effect is to use a 'dodger'—a mask with which to hold back the light. Incidentally, photopaque and other similar products are made with a coarsely ground pigment which is abrasive, so do not use your best airbrush for spraying it.

It may be desirable to reduce highlights on a negative. This can be done by judiciously scraping off the emulsion with a sharp scalpel or needle point. Another method is to rub the highlight area with metal polish which, being abrasive, reduces the density. Local or overall reduction can be obtained with 'Farmer's Solution' which is a mixture of non-acid hypo and potassium ferricyanide (very poisonous). This solution can be applied with cotton wool or a brush, and will reduce the density of the image on the negative. A dish of clean water should be ready in which to immerse the negative in order to halt the chemical action. Farmer's Solution is also used for local or overall density reduction on photoprints. None of these methods should be attempted by the unskilled on a valuable negative or print, and the Farmer's Solution should be safely disposed of and the dish thoroughly washed in running water.

To partially remove shadows on the negative such as skin creases, a retouching medium can be applied with a piece of clean, soft material to the emulsion side. Do not use cotton wool as some of the tiny fibres may stick to the negative. Apply the liquid thinly and evenly, using a circular motion, over the whole area of the emulsion. Do it quickly, because the medium soon dries and, if applied slowly, 'drag marks' may appear. This medium provides a 'tooth' which will accept the graphite of a pencil lightly applied in tiny lines or dots, gradually building up the required density. Remember, the black of the pencil will appear white on the positive photoprint. Work on negatives should be undertaken over a lightbox. It is relatively easy to make your own simple lightbox. A magnifying glass is useful. Do not let the negative get hot or the emulsion will run.

Retouching colours, tones of grey varying from just off-white to almost black, are so mixed that they match the colour of a black and white photoprint. In order to achieve this match, the grey is slightly on the brownish side. If retouching colours are not available, lamp or process black and process white can be mixed to the required density but, in order to get a correct tonal match with the photoprint, it may be necessary to add a little yellow ochre, sepia, crimson or prussian blue. A straight mixture of lamp black and process white has a blue tint which cannot be picked up by the blockmaker's negative film which is not blue sensitive. If the match looks right to the eye, it can safely be assumed to be correct for the camera. Colour matching is equally important when working on colour photographs.

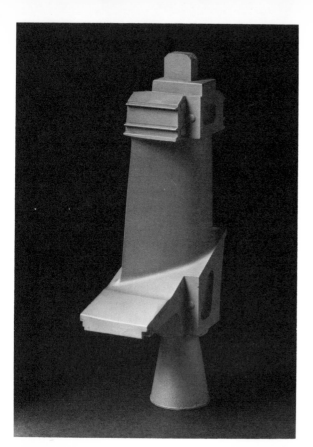

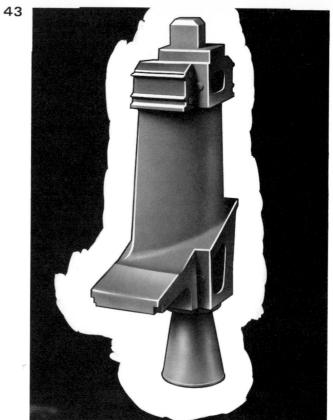

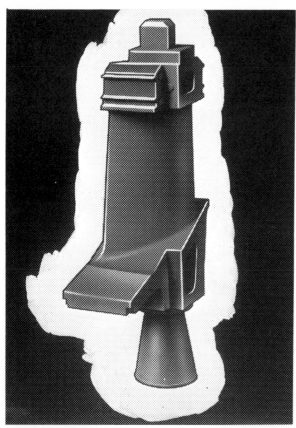

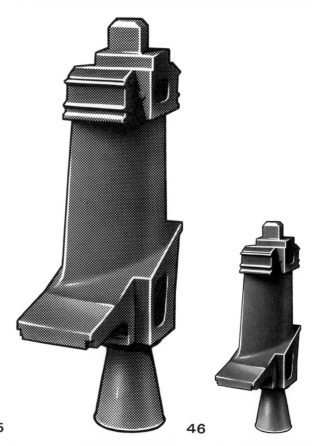

**43-46**  Another effective method of retouching involves quarter-tones. To fully understand the technique it is necessary to know the difference between 'half-tone' and 'line' reproduction which, broadly speaking, can be summed up as follows:

Half-tones — photographs, paintings, drawings with 'continuous tone',
                      finally reproduced with a dot screen in monotone or colour.
Line drawings—drawings which are purely black and white, or solid colours.
From these two different types of artwork, blocks or litho plates are made.

Quarter-tones are a combination of both half-tone and line. First a photograph (43) is retouched (44) or a line and wash drawing is prepared, avoiding small detail and with considerable contrast, the edges being clearly defined. Next a screen negative is made, that is to say, a negative of dots, usually made by the blockmaker. For special effect, or because it is known that the final printing is to be on poor quality or rough paper, or if reproduction is to be by silk screen, the dots can be quite large, of 20 or 30 screen. However, the finished illustration may be in a newspaper printed with a 85-100 screen.

From the screen negative a positive photoprint (45), often referred to as a bromide, is made. Because the image is broken up by the dots, there is a lack of definition, especially in those with a very coarse screen. With the first retouched photograph or line and wash drawing in front of him for reference, the retoucher now works on the screen photoprint putting back detail and edges in black and white only (46). The finished illustration may be reduced in size so that the screen becomes visually finer as shown in illustration 46 and the further reduced example on the immediate left. The finished work is then suitable for line reproduction, but has the merit of containing graduated tones and a very bright contrasty appearance, brought about by virtue of the fact that the blacks and whites are completely black and white and do not have a screen of dots all over them.

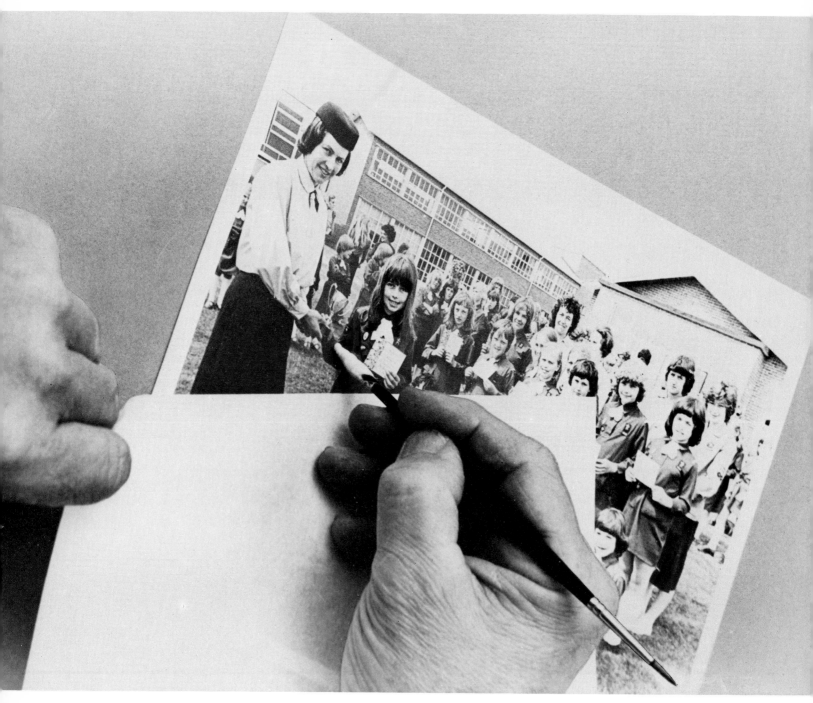

47

# Why retouch?

Retouching may be necessary for a number of reasons, ranging from making an already good photograph suitable for reproduction, to work of a remedial nature. The negative may be damaged or suffer from drying marks, flare, di-chroic fog, uneven development, reticulation, halation or a number of other faults which the retoucher will be asked to remedy on the print. On the other hand, the negative and print may be perfect, but the photograph may contain undesirable features such as telephone wires, trees apparently sprouting from the top of a factory roof, vehicles, people, etc. It may be necessary to remove clouds or put them in, or to spray a flat area in order to make it suitable for overprinting type matter.

Sometimes the retoucher is presented with a photograph of a mock-up or a prototype of a piece of machinery that has rough welding, grease marks, dirty handprints and similar extraneous matter all over it. The floor may be littered with tools and electric cables and the walls hung with papers, oily rags and spare parts. The retoucher's job is to turn this shambles into a freshly painted workshop containing a shining new piece of equipment so that the photograph can be printed in a catalogue in time for the launching of the first production model.

Before starting work on a photograph the retoucher should find out how it is eventually to be used—whether the photoprint is to be mounted or to be cut out and pasted up with other artwork, what screen is to be used. The type of retouching varies with the screen and the screen is determined, especially with letterpress printing, by the type of paper it is to be printed on. If a coarse screen of, say, 65-85 is to be used, a punchy treatment—sometimes referred to as 'soot and whitewash'—is required in order to retain brightness and detail when eventually the image is broken up by the screen. Screens of 100 or more require more subtle work. Having established how the photograph is to be reproduced, the retoucher is ready to start work.

## 47 & 48

Ghosting is a simple, but effective technique where emphasis is required on a selected portion of a photograph—in this case the small girl receiving the cup. A mask can be cut to prevent airbrushing going on to the portion to be given prominence, but usually it is much quicker to airbrush the whole area and then wash off the colour from the emphasised portion with spit-dampened cotton wool on the sharpened end of a brush. Another advantage of the wash-off method is that a softer edge can be obtained than by masking. In this example the child's hair looks more natural than it might have had a mask been used. Where there is small detail the egg masking

medium (see page 43) can be used, but in this example a little strengthening of the silver cup was done with process white and a small touch of lamp black. ·

When ghosting black and white photographs, the grey to be airbrushed can be a mid-tone retouching grey or a mixture of lamp black, process white and a very small proportion of sepia, the latter to offset the blueness of the other two colours. When ghosting is done on a colour photograph, the airbrushed colour should blend with the colour of the photograph, but should have a little process white included in its mix. Remember first of all to make a test to ensure that the watercolour, ink or dye will, in fact, wash off.

Sometimes the photograph will be reproduced as an illustration in a book or magazine, or possibly as part of an advertisement. Where possible, it is advisable to mount the print on board before commencing work. Before mounting the print, look at the back to see the photographer's name, address, telephone number and the negative number. These should be written on the back of the mounting board so that when further copies of the photograph are required, its origin can be traced. This can save a great amount of trouble later on.

Photographs can be mounted with an adhesive photo-mountant but this is inclined, as it dries, to cause the photoprint to contract and, in so doing, cockle the board. Dry mounting is better because the board remains flat. This is done by sandwiching a special tissue between photoprint and board, which are then subjected to pressure in a heated press. Latex gum or latex-based aerosol-spray mountants can also be used, but if the photoprint is non-waterproof, it is liable to lift in places when subjected to long spraying because of the expansion of the print by the water. However, while waterproof prints will not cockle, they have the disadvantage of not readily accepting watercolour paint.

Sometimes it is necessary for a photoprint to be cut to a shape and pasted with other artwork to make a montage design for an advertisement. In this case it is better not to mount the print; instead, if it is non-waterproof, it can be dampened with wet cotton wool or sprayed with clean water. Do this on the back of the print, because the emulsion is liable to damage if allowed to get wet.

Having dampened the print so that it is fairly limp and therefore expanded, stick it down on to a piece of stiff cardboard or hardboard with gummed tape all round the edge of the print—half the width of the tape on the print and half on the board. Watercolour artists do this with cartridge paper before starting work. When the print or paper is dry it will contract, stretch and become flat, so that there is a good smooth surface to work on. Do not use self-adhesive tape, because it will not adhere to the wet print. Waterproof prints do not require dampening. Having completed work on the photoprint, cut the tape to remove the print and then cut it out to the required shape with a scalpel or scissors. If scissors are used, hold the print in a piece of folded paper to avoid damaging the airbrushing.

# Diagnosis of faults

| Airbrushing Fault | Possible Cause | Remedy |
|---|---|---|
| **Coarse spray** | Bent needle | Replace |
| | Damaged nozzle | Replace |
| | Pressure too low | More pressure |
| | Colour too thick | Wash through with clean water or other medium, dilute colour |
| | Needle withdrawn too far for working pressure | Allow needle to move forward, increase pressure, or both |
| **Air blowing back into reservoir causing bubbles** | Aircap not screwed into correct position | Adjust aircap; the orifice of the nozzle should be level with or slightly forward of the hole in the centre of the aircap |
| | Nozzle washer missing | Replace |
| **Little blobs of colour** | Bent needle or damaged nozzle | Replace |
| | Small quantity of colour collected at front of aircap | Partially withdraw needle and wipe out aircap with cotton wool |
| | Needle not sufficiently forward when in closed position | Adjust needle setting; always give trial spray prior to work |
| **Uneven or blobby sprayed surface** | Grease or fingerprints | Wipe over surface with lighter fluid and/or mix ox gall into watercolour. Unsuitable surface such as laminated board will repel colour. Make preliminary test to ensure that colour is compatible with work surface. |
| | Low tack masking film not removed | Check and lift according to area to be airbrushed |

| **Colour will not spray** | Aircap out of position | Adjust or replace |
| | Nozzle washer missing | Replace |
| | Blocked nozzle or reservoir outlet | Partially withdraw needle, clean and spray with clean water, meths, lighter fuel, turpentine or pen-cleaning fluid. If still blocked, with needle partially withdrawn, put finger over aircap, so that air is blown back through nozzle into reservoir. Failing that, where construction allows, remove aircap, nozzle and nozzle washer, hold nozzle up to light to ensure orifice is clear. If not, *do not* poke with pin or needle. Poke from front with hairs of soft brush and then blow from front (see Illustration 8). Ensure that orifice of nozzle is not damaged, by examining under a magnifying glass. Peroxide is also useful in cleaning an airbrush. A well-used nozzle will often wear on one side of the orifice, due to a bent or incorrectly centred needle. This is very likely to happen if coarsely ground colour, which acts as an abrasive, has been sprayed. Replace nozzle or a complete matched set. |

# Airbrush don'ts

**Don't** allow paint or ink to dry in the reservoir.
,, bend the needle point.
,, damage the nozzle orifice.
,, remove the aircap or nozzle without first partially withdrawing the needle.
,, remove the aircap or nozzle without first disconnecting the air hose— if you don't you are liable to blow the nozzle and the nozzle washer across the studio.
,, drop the airbrush.
,, leave the airbrush with colour in it. When work is finished, wash out thoroughly.
,, leave out the airbrush when work is finished. Put it in its case.
,, let children play with the airbrush.
,, scrape out dried colour from the reservoir with anything sharp. Tiny abrasions will make it all the easier for colour to cling and the tiny hard bits can clog the nozzle.
,, lend your airbrush if you can possibly avoid it.

# Not to be taken seriously!

Any airbrusher worth his salt should be able to play The National Anthem on the airbrush. It is done by holding the aircap tightly between forefinger and thumb, letting the air flow and varying the pressure between finger and thumb. After hours of wasted time one can become quite a virtuoso. When you can do it—you are one of us.

Another good time waster is to dance a table tennis ball on the airflow. Just point the airbrush so that the air is blowing upwards. Place the table tennis ball into the airflow and there you are—but don't tell the studio manager that I suggested it!

# Suppliers of airbrushes and accessories

## Airbrushes

| Name | Country of Origin | Agent or Manufacturer | Address |
|---|---|---|---|
| **Efbe** | Germany | Agent: Frisk Products Ltd | 4 Franthorne Way, Randlesdown Road, London SE6 3BT Tel: 01 698 3481/4 |
| **Aerograph** | UK | Manufacturer: The DeVilbiss Co Ltd (Airbrush Division) | 47 Holborn Viaduct, London EC1 Tel: 01 248 4361 |
| **Badger** | UK | Manufacturer: Morris & Ingram (London) Ltd | 156 Stanley Green Rd, Poole, Dorset BH15 3BE Tel: Poole 3757 |
| **Paasche** | USA | Agent: Microflame (UK) Ltd | Abbots Hall, Rickinghall, Diss, Norfolk IP22 1LS |
| | UK | Colour Sprays Ltd | Albion Works, North Road, London N7 |

## Accessories

**Masking fluids**
Maskol—Humbrol
Mastex—Precision Paints
Colorform Resist—Johnsons of London Ltd

**Masking film** (low tack)
Magic Marker
Frisk

**Water colours**
Reeves & Sons Ltd
George Rowney & Co Ltd
Winsor & Newton Ltd
Dr Martins—Distributors: A. Ludwig & Sons Ltd
C. Roberson & Co Ltd

| | |
|---|---|
| **Retouching colours** | Reeves & Sons |
| | George Rowney & Co Ltd |
| | Winsor & Newton Ltd |
| | Schmincke—UK Distributors: Langford & Hill, Graphic House, |
| | 10 Warwick St, nr Regent St, |
| | London W1   Tel: 01 437 0086 |
| | Hunter Penrose |
| | Talens & Zoom—Agents: A. Ludwig & Sons Ltd |
| **Photographic dyes and phototints** | Johnsons of Hendon Ltd |
| | Frisk |
| | Vallego |
| | Westons, Chemists |
| **Inks** | Winsor & Newton Ltd. |
| | Pelican (Germany) |
| **Gum arabic** | Winsor & Newton Ltd |
| **Retouching medium** | Johnsons of Hendon Ltd |
| **Stopping out medium** | Liquid Opaque—Gilbey & Sons Ltd, Devonshire Road, |
| | Colliers Wood, London SW19 |
| **Masking tape** | D.I.Y. shops |
| **Propellents** | Friskair (Frisk) |
| | Speedyspray (Microflame) |
| | Mogramair (Morris & Ingram) |
| **Cutters** | C. W. Edding (UK) Ltd, 49 Corsica St, London N5 |
| | Novaknife—Stanley Tools |
| | Letraset |
| **Scalpels** | Swann-Morton |
| **Stencil patterns** | Morris & Ingram |
| **Pen cleaner** | UNO Pen Cleaner—A. West & Partners Ltd |
| **Rubber solution adhesive** | Cow—Li-lo Ltd, Woking, Surrey |
| | Versifix—Rexel Ltd, Gatehouse Rd, Aylesbury, Bucks, HP19 3DT |